FACE PAINTING TIPS AND HINTS

There are over forty fantastic faces
for you to paint in this book, some really
simple, others a little more complicated.
They are just a starting point. You can
either follow the step-by-step instructions
exactly, or you can use their ideas
to make up your own special faces
or designs, using your own choice
of different colors.

You can buy the make-up and extras from most
craft and hobby shops or where cosmetics or
costumes are sold.

ACKNOWLEDGMENTS

Designed and illustrated by Mei Lim
Photographs by Peter Millard
Make-up artist - Jacqueline Russon
Make-up artist's assistant - Sandy Moir

Created by Thumbprint Books

Library of Congress Cataloging-in-Publication Data Available

2 4 6 8 10 9 7 5 3 1

Published 1994 by Sterling Publishing Company, Inc.
387 Park Avenue South, New York, N.Y. 10016
Originally published in Great Britain by
Hamlyn Children's Books, part of Reed International Books
Michelin House, 81 Fulham Road, London SW3 6RB

© 1994 by Thumbprint Books
Distributed in Canada by Sterling Publishing
c/o Canadian Manda Group, One Atlantic Group, Suite 105
Toronto, Ontario, Canada M6K 3E7

Printed and bound in Italy

Sterling ISBN 0-8069-0929-3

The author would like to thank all the children photographed for this book.

MAKING FACES

CONTENTS

CANCEL

JACQUELINE RUSSON

Sterling Publishing Co., Inc. New York

FACE PAINTS

It's not expensive to buy a basic face painting set. You only need a few colors and two brushes to start with. If you get really interested, you can slowly build up your equipment.

BRUSHES

You will need a small brush for painting outlines and little details, and bigger ones for filling in larger areas. Remember to wash out your brushes thoroughly before painting on each new color.

If you can afford it, it's best to buy real make-up brushes. You can use ordinary paintbrushes instead, but make sure they are not too hard; otherwise they will scratch the skin. Sometimes you may prefer to use your fingers, or you can use sponge eyeshadow applicators.

PAINTS

All the faces in this book have been painted with **water-based** make-up that can be bought either in a palette or in individual containers. It washes off easily with soap and water and suits most people, as it is designed for sensitive skin. It is best never to paint over cuts, rashes or broken skin. Always test for allergic reactions. If paint gets in your eyes, wash it out with cold water.

The colors can be mixed together to give all sorts of interesting shades. Practice mixing some of the colors to see what you can create. Below are some basic combinations for you to try.

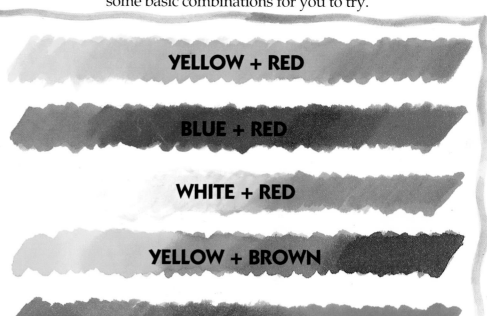

YELLOW + RED

BLUE + RED

WHITE + RED

YELLOW + BROWN

RED + GREEN

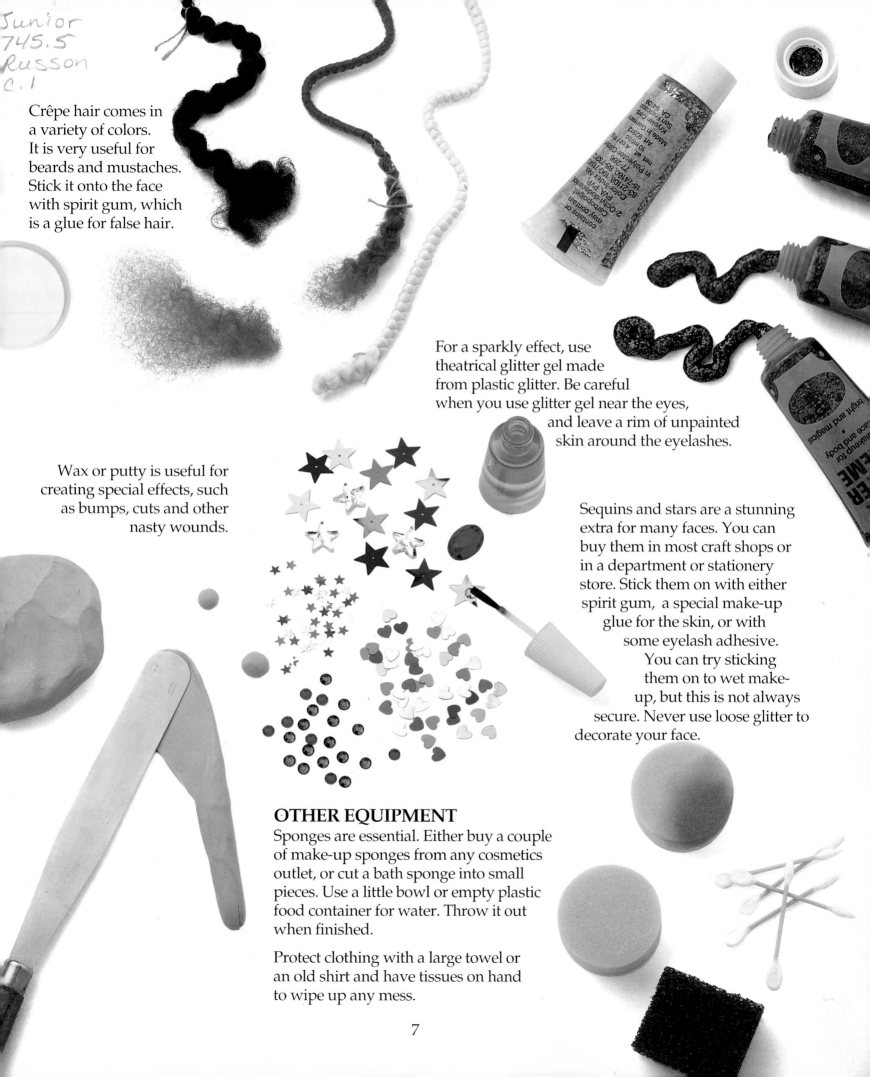

Crêpe hair comes in a variety of colors. It is very useful for beards and mustaches. Stick it onto the face with spirit gum, which is a glue for false hair.

For a sparkly effect, use theatrical glitter gel made from plastic glitter. Be careful when you use glitter gel near the eyes, and leave a rim of unpainted skin around the eyelashes.

Wax or putty is useful for creating special effects, such as bumps, cuts and other nasty wounds.

Sequins and stars are a stunning extra for many faces. You can buy them in most craft shops or in a department or stationery store. Stick them on with either spirit gum, a special make-up glue for the skin, or with some eyelash adhesive. You can try sticking them on to wet make-up, but this is not always secure. Never use loose glitter to decorate your face.

OTHER EQUIPMENT

Sponges are essential. Either buy a couple of make-up sponges from any cosmetics outlet, or cut a bath sponge into small pieces. Use a little bowl or empty plastic food container for water. Throw it out when finished.

Protect clothing with a large towel or an old shirt and have tissues on hand to wipe up any mess.

FIRST STEPS

Before you start face painting, you need to know how to put paint onto the face and how to blend colors together. Use a sponge to put a base coat all over the face and a paintbrush to outline and fill in any small details.

EYES

Be very careful when you paint close to someone's eyes. When you paint the eyes, make sure they are closed but not screwed up . Paint the eyelids first and let them dry.

Make sure that the eyes are looking away from the paintbrush when you paint under or all around them. Too much blinking will smudge the paint.

USING A SPONGE

Wet the sponge. Squeeze it until there are no more drips. Dip it into the paint. Test the wetness on the back of your hand. If the sponge is too wet, the paint may streak.

Start sponging the middle of the face and then around the edges. Sponge the eyes last, which should always be closed.

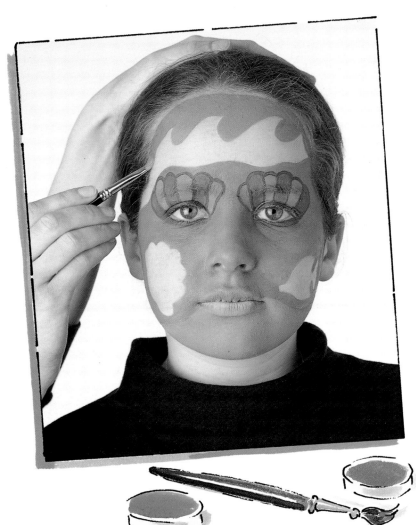

USING A BRUSH

When you paint a shape or a line, try to be as confident about it as you can. Keep the brush moving all the time, so you make a steady line rather than a wobbly one!

If the brush is too dry, it will drag on the skin. If it is too wet, the paint will run. It takes a bit of practice to paint lines that are really smooth. Keep trying!

HAIR COLORING

It is very easy to color hair with water-based make-up. First comb it into the style you want. Then dip a sponge into some paint and press it all over the hair to cover it completely. Use a brush to paint on patterns and an old toothbrush for blobs or streaks. Or you could also use a brightly colored hairspray instead.

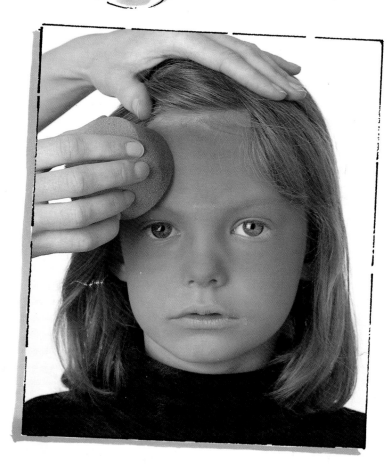

BLENDING

To get a softer or shaded look, it is best to blend colors together. Sponge on the base coat first and let it dry. Then wet and squeeze out a sponge and dip it into the color you want. Gently dab it on to the face, making sure you don't sponge off the base color at the same time.

THE TOY BOX

Here are two easy faces to start off with. Wear bright, spotted or striped clothes and put on a crazy, woolly wig if you have one.

JACK-IN-THE-BOX

1. Sponge a flesh pink base all over the face. Dab big red spots on the cheeks and one on the tip of the nose, like this.

2. Paint a big blue arch over and above both eyelids, covering the eyebrows. Fill them in. Use a fine brush to color in black eyebrows.

3. Color in wide red lips. Paint stars and dots above the cheeks. Outline the arches in blue glitter gel. Add red glitter gel to the cheeks.

Jack-in-the-box bow tie

Cut a rectangle, 5 inches wide and 8 inches long, from thin orange cardboard. Fold the cardboard over along the long edge by ³/₄ of an inch (a). Fold it again, the opposite way. Keep folding it like an accordian (b), until you reach the end. Pinch in the middle and glue a strip of green felt around it. Fan out both sides and decorate them with white paper spots (c). Glue on a piece of thin elastic to fit around your neck (d).

Star tip
To make a star easily, first paint a triangle. Paint another one on top of it, but this time upside down.

10

Costumes

Jack-in-the-box: *Green turtleneck top, spotted bow tie, wool wig, floppy hat with a bell*

Dainty doll: *Braided hair, colorful ribbon bows, pretty dress or shirt and skirt, vest*

DAINTY DOLL

Paint red cheeks and lips and lilac eyelids. Use a very fine brush to paint on black eyelashes under the eyes. For freckles, touch the skin lightly with the tip of a thin paintbrush covered with brown paint.

HOT DOG

Here's a really effective but simple dog face to paint. Instead of making it yellow, brown and white, you could try painting a black and white or just a brown and white doggy face. Remember to keep your hand as steady as possible when you use the paintbrushes.

COLORS
White • Yellow
Brown • Dark brown
Black • Red

1. Paint the outline of the muzzle down the middle of the face using white paint. Fill it in with a big, fat brush. Let the paint dry.

2. Mix yellow with a little brown to get a sandy color. Paint the rest of the face with it. Use a fine brush to paint in thin, black eyebrows.

3. Paint a dark brown spot around each eye. When they are dry, outline the eyes in black with a fine brush. Use the tip to paint black whisker spots around the mouth.

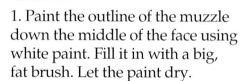

Hot dog ears

Cut four long ear shapes out of light brown fuzzy fabric (a). Put the fuzzy sides of two ear shapes together and sew them, leaving a small opening at the top (b). Do the same with the other two fuzzy ear shapes. Turn both ears inside out, so the fuzz is on the outside. Then wrap the open ends around a plastic hair-band and stitch them together securely (c).

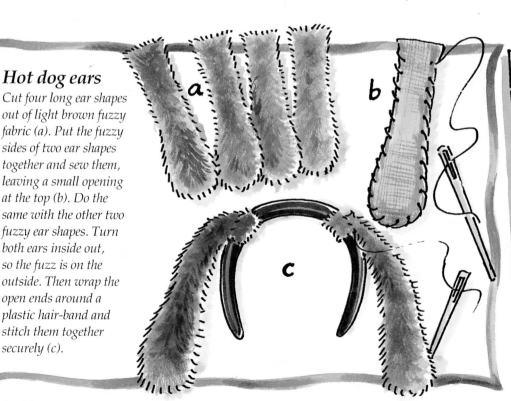

4. Carefully paint the tip of the nose a shiny black. Then, using a thin brush, paint a bright red tongue hanging out of the hot dog's mouth.

Costume
*Hot dog ears,
sandy colored or yellow
turtleneck top,
sandy colored or yellow tights,
fuzzy fabric tail*

WHAT A FACE!

These fun-to-do ideas are for people who want to paint their faces without having to dress up as well. Try painting the designs shown here and then think up your own.

FLOWERS

1. Sponge pink all over one side of the face. Blend in a little red around the outside.

2. Paint different colored flowers on top of the cheek and outline them in black. Put a blob of silver glitter in the middle of each flower.

BATTY BATS

1. Carefully sponge orange all over the face. Blend a little red around the outside.

2. Paint spooky little black bats on the forehead and cheeks.

3. Paint a gold glitter gel circle for the sun. Outline it in black.

SLITHERY SNAKE

1. Sponge yellow all over one side of the face. Blend light green around the outside.

2. Paint a green snake with black scales. Outline it in black.

3. Paint a white and black eye and a red forked tongue.

SPOOKY SPIDER

1. Sponge orange all over one side of the face.

2. Starting with the outside line, paint a delicate spider's web with a thin brush.

3. Paint a big black blob in the middle of the web for the spider's body and a smaller one for its head. Paint on eight legs.

4. Add silver glitter gel to make the web sparkle.

Star tip

Always use a fine brush to paint little designs. Allow each color to dry before painting on the next one.

STARS AND MOONS

Sponge blue all over the face. Paint yellow stars and a white moon on the forehead and cheeks.

HEARTS

1. Sponge white all over one side of the face. Blend in a little pink around the outside.

2. Paint big and little red hearts on the cheek. Outline them in black. Decorate with silver glitter gel.

PLUNDERING PIRATES

Paint a mean pirate face with lots of stubble on the cheeks and chin, a skull and crossbones and a nasty-looking scar. Then put on a black eye patch and go hunting for treasure on a desert island. Or dress up as an evil pirate captain with a ruffled shirt, a plumed hat and a big, swirly mustache.

COLORS
Light and dark brown
Black • Red • White

CRUEL CAPTAIN
Sponge a light brown base all over the face. Then paint or stick on an enormous mustache. If you can get hold of one, a long, curly wig looks really effective.

Star tip
Dip an old toothbrush into some black paint. Run it through the eyebrows to make them dark and bushy.

Black eye patch

Cut a big eye patch shape from a piece of cardboard. Cut another slightly larger one from black fabric (a). Glue this to the eye patch, folding over and sticking down the edges (b). Snip a small hole in either side. Thread a thin piece of elastic through the holes, long enough to fit around your head. Knot the ends together (c).

FIRST MATE

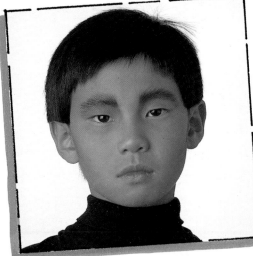

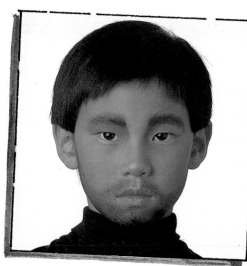

1. Sponge a light brown base all over the face to give a tanned look. Blend dark brown under the cheekbones and around the eyes. Paint bushy black eyebrows.

2. Sponge black around the chin and over the top lip. Dip an old tooth-brush in black paint. Dab it lightly over the black to give a stubble effect. Sponge red over the cheeks.

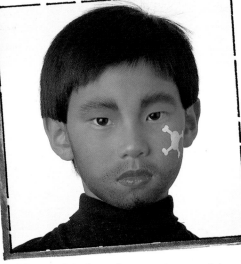

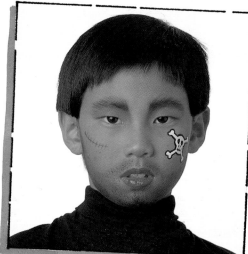

3. Use a thin brush to paint a white skull and crossbones shape on one cheek, like this. Then color the lips a ruddy red.

4. Outline the skull and crossbones in black and paint in the face of the skull. Paint a thin black scar on the other cheek, as shown.

Costumes

First mate: Eye patch, spotted scarf, magnetic or clip-on earring, striped T-shirt, vest

Cruel captain: Black hat, long, curly wig or curled hair, frilly shirt, long jacket, mustache, treasure map

17

MASKED BALL

In New Orleans, during Mardi Gras, people wear masks like these to disguise themselves. Try painting your own sparkly mask – a Harlequin or a butterfly mask – decorated with glittering gold.

COLORS
Pink • Purple • Green
Black • Orange • Lilac
Red • Dark blue • Sequins
Gold glitter gel • Shiny stars

SPARKLY MASK

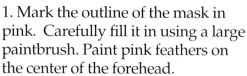

1. Mark the outline of the mask in pink. Carefully fill it in using a large paintbrush. Paint pink feathers on the center of the forehead.

2. Stick on shiny stars or sequins before the paint dries. Paint green and purple feathers in between the pink ones.

Costumes
Sparkly mask: *Long dress, pink feather boa, jeweled choker*
Butterfly: *Leotard, tights and chiffon scarf*
Harlequin: *Black cloak, white ruff, black leggings and boots, harlequin hat*

3. Outline the edges of the mask and the feathers with gold glitter gel. Color the lips pink. Paint a black beauty spot on one cheek.

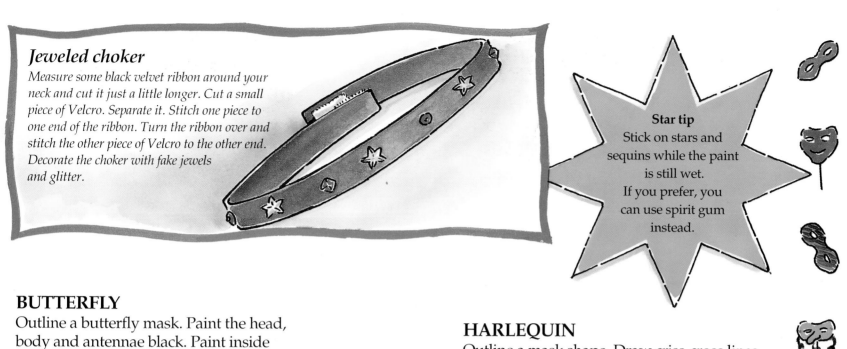

Jeweled choker

Measure some black velvet ribbon around your neck and cut it just a little longer. Cut a small piece of Velcro. Separate it. Stitch one piece to one end of the ribbon. Turn the ribbon over and stitch the other piece of Velcro to the other end. Decorate the choker with fake jewels and glitter.

Star tip
Stick on stars and sequins while the paint is still wet. If you prefer, you can use spirit gum instead.

BUTTERFLY

Outline a butterfly mask. Paint the head, body and antennae black. Paint inside the wings in different colors. Outline the sections and decorate the body, wings and antennae with gold glitter gel.

HARLEQUIN

Outline a mask shape. Draw criss-cross lines inside the mask, so that you make rows of diamonds. Paint the diamonds red and blue. Outline the mask with gold glitter.

ALL BEAR

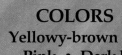

Why not have a teddy bears' picnic with your friends and each paint your face as a different sort of bear? You could be a grizzly bear, a panda or just a cuddly teddy bear.

COLORS
Yellowy-brown
Pink • Dark brown
Black • White

TEDDY BEAR

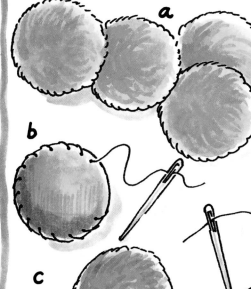

Teddy bear ears
Draw and cut out four brown fuzzy fabric circles, each about 4 inches in diameter (a). Put the fuzzy sides of two circles together and sew them, leaving a small opening (b). Do the same with the other two circles. Turn both ears inside out, so the fuzz is on the outside. Stuff them with cotton wool (c). Sew the openings securely together over a plastic hair-band. Paint the center of both the ears a very dark brown (d).

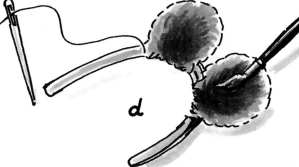

1. Sponge a yellow-brown base all over the face. Very carefully blend pink into the cheeks.

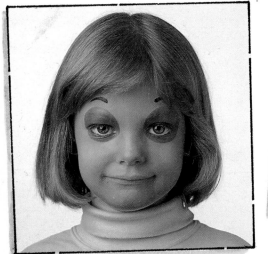

Costumes
Teddy bear: Yellowy-brown top and tights, teddy bear ears
Panda: Black turtleneck top and tights, black ears

2. Paint a big dark brown circle around each eye. Using a fine brush, paint two black eyebrows.

3. Paint a black nose and a thick line from the tip of the nose to the top lip. Paint a smiley teddy bear mouth and add little black whisker spots.

PANDA

Follow the same basic steps as the teddy bear,
but use two coats of white base instead of
a yellow-brown one. Paint a black nose
and mouth, thin eyebrows
and big black eyes.

Star tip

When you paint your
nose, start on one side.
Keep the brush on the skin
and paint over to the other
side all in one go.
This helps to stop the
paint from smudging.

OUT OF THIS WORLD

Do you and your friends want to look weird and mysterious, as if you come from another planet? If so, then these faces are just the thing. Complete the effect by painting your hair and hands as well as your face. Stick on some glitter and shiny stars.

Alien antennae

Pour green glitter into a saucer. Cover two Ping Pong balls with glue (a). Roll them in the glitter (b). Then cut two 8 inch lengths of green garden wire. Wind them round a pencil, like this, to curl them (c). Pierce a hole in each ball and push in one end of the wire. Seal the holes with a blob of glue (d). Wrap the other ends of the wire tightly around a plastic hair band (e).

Star tip

If you want a really shiny flash, cut one out of silver paper and stick it to your cheek with spirit gum or some eyelash adhesive.

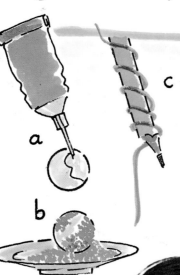

SPACE CADET

Sponge a white base all over the face. Paint the eyelids and lips shocking pink. Color in two black eyebrows. Shade the cheeks and outline the eyes and lips in purple. Stick shiny green stars under the eyebrows.

AWESOME ALIEN

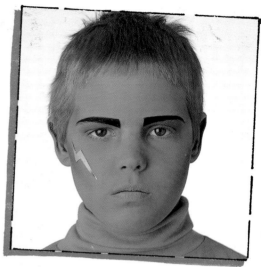

Costumes

Awesome alien: Green turtleneck top and tights, green antennae, purple and orange hair

Space cadet: Silver top, red or purple tights, pink and purple hair

1. Sponge a bright green base all over the face. Blend dark green under the cheekbones and on the eyelids. Color the ears and neck as well.

2. Paint or stick a silver flash across one cheek. Paint the eyebrows black.

3. Line the eyes with dark green. Put green glitter gel over the eyelids and up to the painted eyebrows.

4. Stick silver stars above one cheek bone. Paint green glitter gel on the lips.

TIGER TROUBLE

If you're feeling fierce and ferocious, why not paint these fabulous faces of fearsome creatures? Then stalk through the house or garden, growling greedily.

SPOTTED LEOPARD
Sponge a yellow base all over the face. Paint a spiked white fan shape above the eyelids and white lines on either side of the nose. Use your fingers to dab on brown and black spots. Add a pink nose. Outline the eyes and nose in black. Add a thick black mouth.

Costumes
Fuzzy ears on headbands (see page 20), orange, yellow or black turtleneck top and matching tights

LAZY LION
Follow the same steps as the tiger, but use a yellow base with brown blended around the outside. Paint black and brown stripes around the face. Outline the eyes in black. Add a thick black mouth.

TERRIBLE TIGER

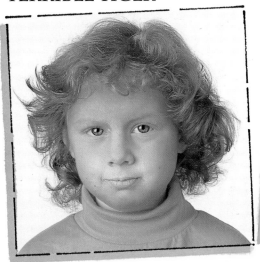

1. Sponge a yellow base all over the face. Blend orange and red around the outside and down the nose, and white on either side of the mouth.

2. Paint a spiked white fan shape above each eyelid, as shown. Paint some long, pointed white stripes around the outside of the face.

3. Paint pointed black stripes between the white ones. Color the end of the nose pink.

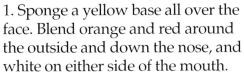

4. Paint a snarling black tiger's mouth. Outline the nose in black and add black whisker spots on either side of the mouth.

Star tip
Paint the hair with the same brush and colors you use for the face. Add spots for the leopard and stripes for the tiger.

WHAT A PICTURE!

On a rainy day, why not paint one of these sunny scenes to make your friends smile? Once you've mastered the technique, you could paint any scene you like. How about a garden, a mountaintop or a rocky shore?

EGYPTIAN SUNSET

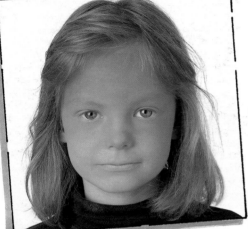

1. Sponge red over the forehead, orange over the eyebrows and down to the tip of the nose, and yellow over the mouth, lower cheeks and chin. Blend one color into another, using a damp sponge (see First Steps on page 8).

2. Paint a black sand dune over the lower half of the face, like this. Then very carefully outline the eyes in black, using a fine brush.

3. Paint two solid-gold pyramids standing on the black sand dune. Outline them in black. Paint a gold sun in the middle of the forehead.

4. Paint black palm trees on either side of the pyramids and some black birds flying in the sky.

Black wool wig

Cut the peak off an old baseball cap (a). Snip a ball of black wool into lots of 12-inch lengths. Smear lines of glue from the crown of the cap to its rim and stick on the lengths of wool, one by one (b). When the cap is covered with wool, stick on another layer. Trim the ends, so that they are the same length all the way around. Cut a fringe (c). Wrap gold braid around the wig and stitch or glue the ends together (d).

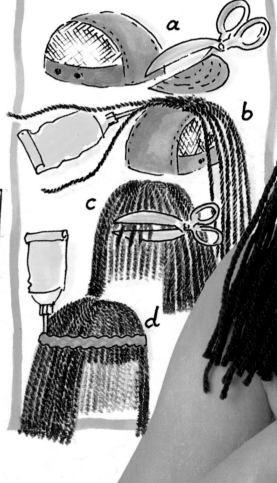

26

Costumes

Egyptian sunset: *Black wool wig, white sheet or long, black dress*

Tropical island: *Blue turtleneck top, or bathing suit and sun hat*

TROPICAL ISLAND

Follow the same order of steps as for the Egyptian sunset, but use light blue for the sky, dark blue for the sea and yellow for the sand. Paint two big green and brown palm trees and lots of white gulls flying in the sky.

Star tip

Use the tip of a small, thin brush to paint fine details, such as the flying birds, or to outline the eyes.

DREADFUL DINOSAUR

Professional make-up artists use lots of tricks to create particular effects. They use a special kind of wax or putty to make warts, lumps and bumps. Try making a lumpy, bumpy brow bone on this dreadful dinosaur face and amaze your family and friends.

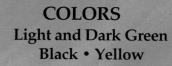

COLORS
Light and Dark Green
Black • Yellow

1. Carefully dab spirit gum above the eyebrows, making sure the eyes are shut. Form a big lump of wax into a brow bone shape. Press it onto the spirit gum and hold for a few seconds. Blend the edges of the wax into the skin with a spatula.

2. Sponge a light green base all over the face, being careful not to disturb the waxy brow bone. Sponge yellow over the wax, cheeks and chin, and down the sides of the nose.

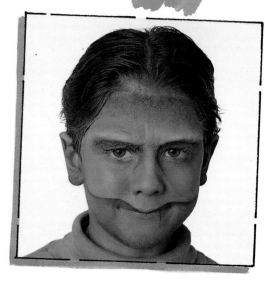

3. Blend dark green into the eye sockets and down the sides of the nose. Paint on a dark green dinosaur mouth. Then soften the line with a dry sponge.

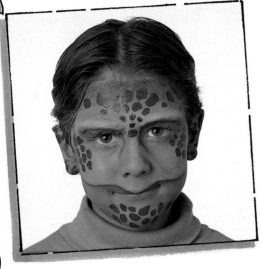

4. Use dark green to paint dinosaur scales all over the forehead, cheeks and chin. Make them different shapes and sizes, like this.

5. Outline the eyes in black and smudge them with a dry brush. Paint in two dinosaur nostrils. Color the hair green to match the dreadful dinosaur's face.

Star tip
Don't handle the wax too much or it will get sticky and difficult to use. Try not to put it on movable parts of the face.

28

Dinosaur horns

Cut out four large and two small horn shapes from green felt (a). Stitch pairs of matching shapes together to make three horns (b). Turn them inside out and stuff them with cotton (c). Paint scales on the two big horns to match the face. Then stitch them onto a plastic headband (d). Stitch a length of thin, black elastic to the smaller horn, big enough to go around your head (e). Paint scales on the horn (f).

Things you need
*Spatula or palette knife
Theatrical wax or putty
Spirit gum (soluble if possible)
Moisturizing cream*

CRAZY CLOWNS

Everybody loves the funny face of a clown. Here's how to paint two completely different happy, laughing clowns. Now all you need to do is learn some silly tricks!

COLORS
Red • Green • Orange
Black • Yellow • Purple
Green and red glitter gel

SMILING CLOWN

1. Sponge a bright red circle on each cheek and a little red on the tip of the nose. Color in enormous upturned red lips, like this.

2. Paint a green arch above one eye and an orange triangle under it. Paint an orange arch over the other eye and a green triangle under it.

3. With a small brush, paint thin, black eyebrows. Outline the orange and green arches in black. Paint stars and dots on the cheeks.

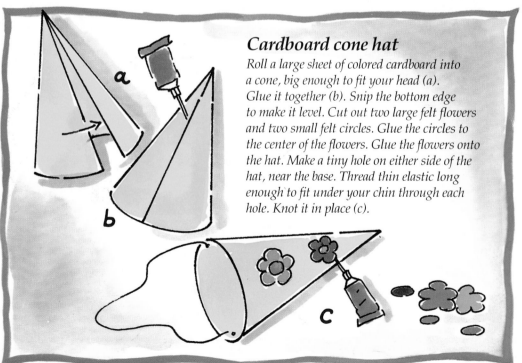

Cardboard cone hat

Roll a large sheet of colored cardboard into a cone, big enough to fit your head (a). Glue it together (b). Snip the bottom edge to make it level. Cut out two large felt flowers and two small felt circles. Glue the circles to the center of the flowers. Glue the flowers onto the hat. Make a tiny hole on either side of the hat, near the base. Thread thin elastic long enough to fit under your chin through each hole. Knot it in place (c).

Costumes
Smiling clown: *Bowler hat, wig, oversized shirt, baggy trousers and suspenders, spotted bow tie*
Glitter clown: *Cardboard cone hat, ruff, T-shirt, baggy trousers, brightly colored wig*

30

Star tip

Give happy clowns upturned lips and sad clowns downturned lips.

GLITTER CLOWN

Paint the nose, cheeks and lips red as you would for a smiling clown. Paint a different colored diamond shape over each eye. Add glitter gel to the diamonds and the red cheek spots. To make the clown look even more sparkly, stick sequins or stars on the cheekbones.

COPY CATS

For a really unusual effect, paint your face to match your clothes. It's best to choose a strongly patterned top or one with a picture. Wild T-shirts are great.

COLORS
Use the paints that match the colors of your top as closely as possible.

STRIPED FACE

1. Mark out the stripy pattern on the face using a watery white paint.

2. Color in thick red and pink stripes with a big brush.

3. Use a fine brush to paint thinner green and blue stripes.

WHAT A PICTURE!

1. Mark out the pattern of the shirt on the face with watery white paint.

2. Paint in the details, such as flowers and leaves, in the same colors as the top.

3. Paint in the background color. Using a thin brush, outline and highlight the details you want.

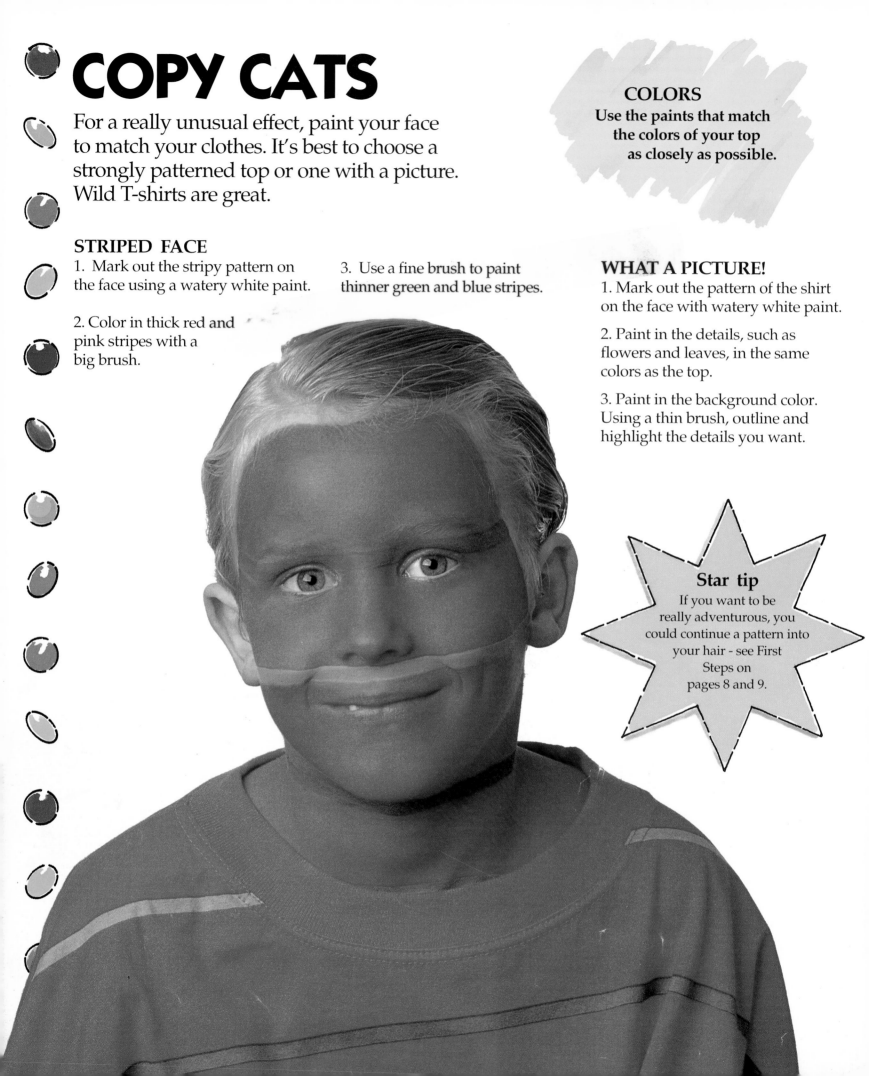

Star tip
If you want to be really adventurous, you could continue a pattern into your hair - see First Steps on pages 8 and 9.

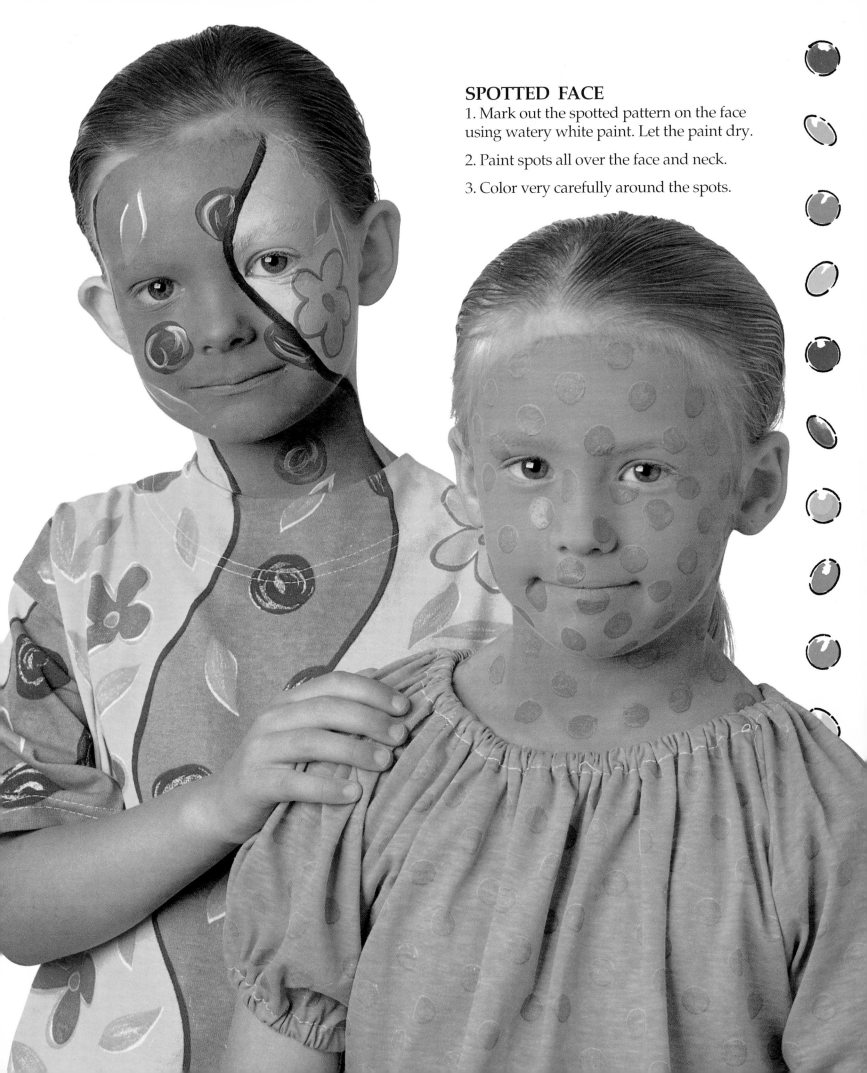

SPOTTED FACE

1. Mark out the spotted pattern on the face using watery white paint. Let the paint dry.

2. Paint spots all over the face and neck.

3. Color very carefully around the spots.

RABBIT, RABBIT

The good thing about face painting is that it doesn't have to be too true to life. Instead of painting an ordinary brown rabbit, why not paint a glittery pink one or a classy gray and white magician's rabbit. He could wear a black jacket and a tall top hat.

COLORS
Pale pink • Lilac • Black
Dark pink • Red • White
Light gray • Dark gray
Silver glitter gel

PINK RABBIT

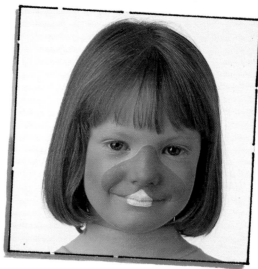

1. Sponge a pale pink base all over the face. Blend dark pink into both cheeks to make them rosy-red.

2. Use the same dark pink to paint a rabbit's muzzle, like this. Paint a blob of white for the teeth.

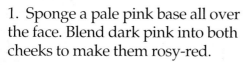

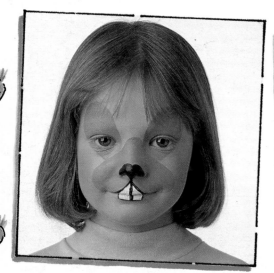

3. Use black to paint the tip of the nose and to outline the muzzle and teeth. Use a fatter brush to paint a lilac oval around each eye.

4. Paint on thick black eyebrows, thin whiskers and whisker spots. Dab silver glitter gel onto the cheeks.

Rabbit ears

Cut out four rabbit ears from dark pink felt. Glue thin wire down the middle of two of them (a). Glue a second ear shape on top of each of the wired ears. Leave the bottom edges open. Cut out two smaller ears from light pink felt. Glue one to the middle of each big ear (b). Stick silver glitter around them. Sew the open edges of the ears together over a plastic headband (c).

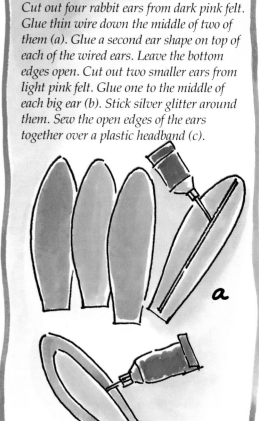

MAGICIAN'S WHITE RABBIT

Follow the same steps as the pink rabbit, using white
for the base, light gray for the muzzle and dark gray
for the eyes. Paint the tip of the nose red. Paint a red
heart on one cheek and
a black diamond on
the other.

Star tip
To add that extra
sparkle, use different
colored
glitter paints.

WICKED WITCH & WACKY WIZARD

COLORS
Bright green • Gold
Black • Light green
Purple • White • Yellow

Paint your face a spooky green color to turn yourself into this wild and wicked witch. Or become a wacky wizard with a ghostly white face, white hair, a long, straggly beard and mustache, and a patterned gown.

WICKED WITCH

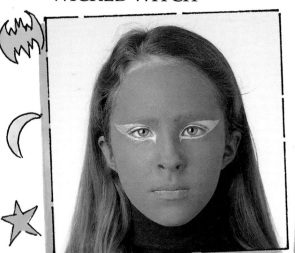

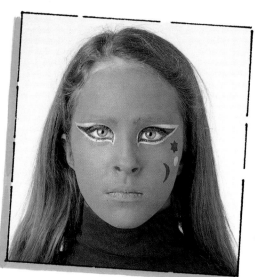

1. Sponge a bright green base all over the face. Paint a leaf shape in gold, like this, over and around the eyes. Make them pointed at both ends.

2. Carefully outline the eyes in black, as shown, using a small, fine brush. Then paint a black star and moon, and a gold sun on one cheek.

3. Paint two long, black pointed eyebrows and a black beauty spot just above the lips. Color the lips a shiny black.

Creepy cloak

Cut a cloak shape out of some black fabric or a black plastic bag. Cut small slits along the top of the cloak and thread some green ribbon through them. Cut out paper moons, stars and bats in different colors. Glue them all over the creepy cloak.

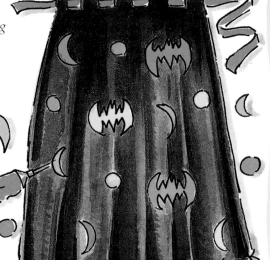

Star tip
You can use black paint to color your fingernails, or wear long, false black nails.

4. Paint a spider's web over the other cheek with a small brush. Start with the outside of the web and work your way into the middle.

WACKY WIZARD

The wizard's face is slightly different from the witch's face. Sponge on a white base and then paint the eyes as shown. Color in a moon and suns in different colors on the cheeks. Outline them in black. Paint the lips a deep purple. Stick on a long, white beard and mustache.

Costumes

Wicked witch: Witch's hat, green wig, creepy cloak, black dress or skirt

Wacky wizard: Pointed hat, straggly wool beard and mustache, long cloak or robe, wand

JUST FOR FUN

Let your imagination take over while you think up some really crazy faces to paint just for fun. These four faces give you an idea of a few unusual and colorful designs to try.

COLORFUL CLOCK

Sponge a white circle over the face. Let it dry. Outline it in black. Paint the 3, 6, 9 and 12, each in a different color. Then space the other numbers between them. Paint the clock hands in black. Remember to make the hour hand a little bit shorter than the minute hand.

CLOUDS AND RAINBOW

Paint three white clouds, one on the forehead and one on each cheek. Then mark out the stripes of the rainbow across the face from one side of the forehead to the top of the cloud on the opposite cheek.

With the eyes closed, fill in the rainbow colors — red, orange, yellow, green, blue, indigo and purple. Blend the edges of the stripes together with a dry brush. Paint the rest of the face blue.

ICE CREAM CONE

Sponge a white base all over the face. Draw the outline of a cone from the eyes to the chin. Paint it sandy yellow. Then add brown criss-cross lines. Paint pink, green and brown ice cream balls on top of the cone with a large brush.

Add dark pink ripples to the pink ice cream and brown chocolate chips to the mint ice cream. Paint a pale brown chocolate wafer and outline it with dark brown.

Star tip
It is best to mark out all your designs with a small brush in watery white before you use any colors.

BRIGHT BALLOONS

Sponge a yellow base all over the face. Then mark out where the balloons will go. Paint them each a different color, as shown. Outline them in black and add a wiggly black string to each one. Paint in some brightly colored streamers.

FAIRYTALE FACES

Paint these fairytale faces with lots of glitter and sparkle. As well as a pixie, a flower fairy and a pretty princess, you could choose your own fairytale characters, such as a haughty snow queen or an evil elf.

COLORS
Pale green • Dark green
Light pink • Dark pink
Yellow • Purple
White • Black
Gold and silver glitter

Flowery headdress

Cut out four small circles all the same size from white tissue. Put them on top of each other and pinch the middles to make a flower shape. Sponge pink paint on the petals (a). Blob glue over them and dip them in silver glitter. To make a stalk, twist a white pipe cleaner under the petals. Make lots of flowers. Wrap the stems around a wire ring or headband to make a flowery headdress (b).

a

b

PRINCESS

Sponge pink on the cheeks. Paint the lips dark pink. Dab silver glitter gel on the eyelids and paint a big black beauty spot above the top lip.

PIXIE

Follow the same steps as the fairy, but use green make-up. Paint yellow dots on the cheeks and dab a little gold glitter on the eyelids and lips.

FABULOUS FAIRY

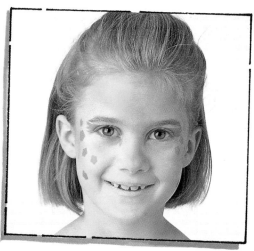

1. Sponge a thin white base all over the face. Blend light pink into the forehead, the tip of the nose and the cheeks. Blend a strip of pale green over the eyes and down the nose, as shown. Color the lips green.

2. Use a dark pink to paint over each eyelid and down into a point at the corner of each eye. Paint pink and green flowers on the cheeks.

3. Paint pointed dark green eyebrows. Use a dry sponge to blend dark green into the pale green. Outline the lips in green. Outline the flowers and color their centers.

Costumes

Fairy: Gathered net skirt, flowery headdress, leotard and wand
Pixie: Leaf collar, top and tights
Princess: Pretty dress and tiara

4. Carefully outline the eyes in purple with a fine brush. Paint purple flowers on the cheeks. Dab silver glitter gel over the eyebrows.

Star tip
To paint a flower make five overlapping circles. Put a blob of color or glitter in the middle.

SPOOKY FACES

Of course you've heard the spooky story of Count Dracula. Why not paint your face to look just like him and really frighten your friends? Or turn yourself into a ghoulish skeleton with a scary skull and a bony body.

Bony skeleton

To make a skeleton costume, cut bone shapes out of sticky-backed white paper. You'll need rib bones, arm and hand bones, leg and feet bones, and hip bones. Stick them on to a black turtleneck top and black tights or leggings. Wear black gloves with bones stuck on them.

SCARY SKULL

Cover the hair with the top of a black stocking or a black or white bathing cap. Sponge a white base all over the face. Paint black around the eyes, on the nose, chin and down the sides of the face, as shown. Paint the middle of the lips black, and add thin black teeth, while the mouth is closed.

Star tip

Buy fake blood from a theater supply or toy shop. Use it to look as if you've just taken a monster bite.

DREADFUL DRACULA

1. Sponge a thin, white ghoulish base all over the face. Use a small sponge to blend gray under the cheek bones and chin, as shown.

2. Blend gray around the eyes, down the nose and on the temples, using a damp sponge. Outline the eyes in red. Smudge them with a dry sponge .

3. Paint the lips purple and the eyebrows black. Use a thin brush to paint black frown lines between the eyebrows, like this.

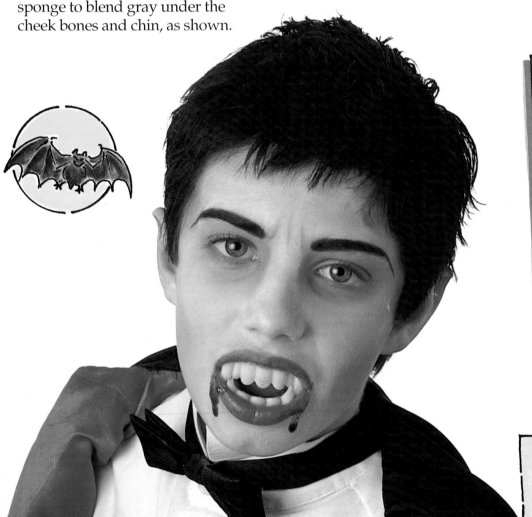

4. Color the hair with thick black water-color paint. Then trickle drops of fake blood or red paint from the corners of the mouth.

Costumes

Dracula: Black cloak, white shirt, bow tie, fake fangs and blood
Scary skull: Black stocking top, black turtleneck top, tights and gloves with bones stuck on

FISH FACE

Think about all the beautiful patterns of shells, fish and seaweed when you paint this incredible underwater fishy face. You could add all sorts of other watery creatures, such as a starfish, a jellyfish, a seahorse or even an octopus.

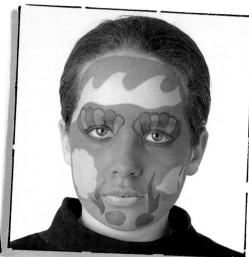

COLORS
Turquoise • Orange • White
Sandy yellow • Black • Brown
Dark and light green
Dark and pale pink

1. Use white paint to mark out foaming waves, shell shapes and a big fish, in the positions shown. Paint in the turquoise sea around the shapes. Paint the chin and bottom lip a sandy color.

2. Fill in the shell shapes over the eyes with alternating stripes of dark and light green. Outline the shells and the eyes in dark green.

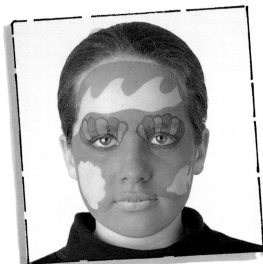

3. With a small brush, paint the shell on the cheek pale pink. Paint two brown stones on the sand and add some wiggly green seaweed.

Star tip
Blend the outlines of the eyes and the shells with a dry brush to give them a softer look.

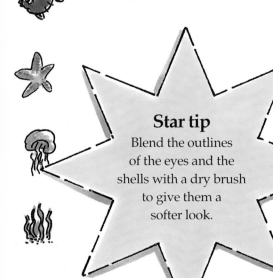

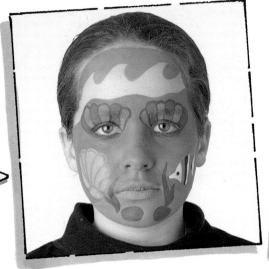

4. Outline the pink shell in darker pink. Paint orange, white and black stripes on the fish. Color in its eye.

5. Outline the fish in black with a fine brush. Use white paint to fill in the foaming waves on the forehead.

Costume
Turquoise turtleneck or off-the-shoulder top, shell necklace, wig set in curls and decorated with shells

INDEX